Penn State
Then and Now

To: Diane & Gary Slatt,

We are . . . Penn State!

Best Wishes,

Pat Little
12-18-99

by Pat Little

ISBN 0-9670580-0-7
copyright Pat Little 1999
copyright The Pennsylvania
State University 1999

Published by:
Pat Little Photography
P.O. Box 627
Lemont, PA 16851

10987654321
First Edition July, 1999
Original concept, photography and layout
Pat Little
Word Editors:
B.J. Clitherow
Mike Joseph
Penn State Archives:
Jackie Esposito
Lee Stout
Cover Design:
K.C. Murphy
Printed in the U.S.A. by
Precision Book and Litho
Philipsburg, PA
Bound in the U.S.A. by
Jostens Commercial Printing & Publishing
State College, PA

Introduction

"Townie." I was 11 or 12 at the time and I remember how weird that sounded. The students at Penn State had a name for the town's people. The line was always "You actually live here? Nobody lives here, do they? Are your parents professors?" Yes, people do live here, and here is the secret.... they love it. So did the students who passed through this special place we call Penn State. With the construction of record numbers of retirement villages and the ever-expanding State College area, a lot of people are returning to Penn State. You'll note that I refer to State College and Penn State interchangeably. For us who live and work here it has always been that way. They are forever locked in a dance of destiny. This book is called <u>Penn State Then and Now</u>. It could have been called <u>State College and Penn State Then and Now</u>, but that wasn't feasible. So it's <u>Penn State Then and Now</u> with a lot of State College photographs.

 I grew up around Penn State and my career, as a photographer, began with *The Daily Collegian* in 1977. For the past 17 years I have been recording Penn State and Centre County history as a photojournalist for the *Centre Daily Times*. I have been an eyewitness to the joys and the growing pains of history.

The history of Penn State is like that of the world. We have had our moments and our discoveries. What I have tried to do in these pages is take a look at who we were and who we are. When I was shooting this book I was overwhelmed by my feelings for the people at the turn of the last century. As I looked through the eyes of earlier photographers (see pages for 190-191 for details) I saw people, much like ourselves, going about their business. They had no idea of what the future would bring. At my fingertips I have access to all the knowledge they could have ever imagined. This brought me to the realization that we are at the same place in time as they were. What lies ahead of us? Things we can not even imagine.

I hope you enjoy my look at the past and the present life in Happy Valley. It is my hope that in 50 or 100 years these photographs will give people not born yet a better understanding of who we were. And when a photographer redoes this book and looks through my eyes, I hope he or she feels the connection that I did. It was a pleasure.

Pat Little

Penn State Presidents

Evan Pugh
1859-1864

William H. Allen
1864-1866

John Fraser
1866-1868

Thomas Burrowes
1868-1871

James Calder
1871-1880

Joseph Shortlidge
1880-1881

James McKee
1881-1882**

George Atherton
1882-1906

James A. Beaver
1906-1908**

Edwin E. Sparks
1908-1920

John M. Thomas
1921-1925

Ralph D. Hetzel
1926-1947

James Milholland
1947-1950**

Milton Eisenhower
1950-1956

Eric A. Walker
1956-1970

John W. Oswald
1970-1983

Bryce Jordan
1983-1990

Joab Thomas
1990-1995

Graham Spanier
1995-

** Acting

5

Old Main

1859

Daily chores, in front of the unfinished Old Main: F. Sheraden, Fred Watts,
W. Cottrell. Three hours daily labor was part of the curriculum.

Old Main acquired its name around 1900. It wasn't a chosen name, just a name
that the students and faculty started calling the building because it was the oldest and
main campus building. The building was originally designed to be five stories, with
three sections. However, work was halted in 1858, because of financial difficulties, and
only one third of it stood when the first class -- 69 of the 100 accepted students--
arrived on Feb. 16, 1859, at The Farmer's High School of Pennsylvania.

Penn State's first president, Evan Pugh, used this photograph in an 1861 appeal to the state legislature for funds to complete Old Main. On May 1, 1862, Penn State was renamed the Agricultural College of Pennsylvania.

In 1862, the tuition, room and board was $100 for the year, running from February to December. Old Main was completed in December of 1863.

1865

In February of 1864, 146 students lived in Old Main.

circa 1863

The rear carpenter's shanties were used as dining
halls until the structure was complete.

circa 1865

When completed, Old Main had 64 dorm rooms, six private apartments, two lecture rooms, a library, reading room, chapel, business office and several rooms for chemical, geological & philosophical apparatus. In 1874, the Agricultural College of Pennsylvania was renamed the Pennsylvania State College.

1894

Dr. Fred Lewis Pattee teaches a class in Bibliography (Library Science) in the Library of Old Main. In 1901, he wrote the Alma Mater.

1894

Old Main Chemistry Laboratory.

1894

Electric lights were added in 1887 along with other modern comforts of the time. Here the Washington Literary Society poses for a photo.

1894

The Chapel in the original Old Main.

1894

The stairwell of Old Main "THE WELL" circa 1895

circa 1904
The movements of the Old Main clock.

In the 1880s and 90s all students, except the few residing in or near the village of State College, roomed on the third, fourth and fifth floors of Old Main. The fifth floor was the most popular, owing in part, perhaps, to the fact that here the students had a feeling of superiority, being above everybody else, and in part, perhaps, to the fact that a "poke of water" (paper bag filled with water) had farther to fall on an unsuspecting individual.

Extract from the manuscript of the History of the Pennsylvania State University by Dr. Wayland Dunaway.

circa 1906

The College provided an iron single bed, two chairs, a table, a bureau and wash stand, but no curtains, carpet or bedding were furnished. Two students were usually in each room.

circa 1904

The roof and tower were damaged by fire in 1903. The fire resulted in a new tower and clock for Old Main. The myth is that Old Main was completely destroyed. It wasn't.

circa 1904

Students take in the view from the bell tower.

1929

With walls too weak to permit substantial renovation, Old Main was demolished. The new Old Main was to rise on the same site in a similar architectural style and to incorporate, whenever possible, the stone of the original structure.

August 29, 1929

With the "old" Old Main completely removed, a new Old Main would rise in its place.

February 13, 1930

October 1995

1930

The new Old Main bell tower goes up as the landmark building takes shape.

circa 1935

The new Old Main was designed by Charles Klauder in a Federal Revival style. The building incorporates much of the stone from the original structure. A major share of the stone originally came from a quarry along present day College Avenue. Reopened on the 75th University celebration in October of 1930 the new Old Main came in at a cost of $837,000.

1940

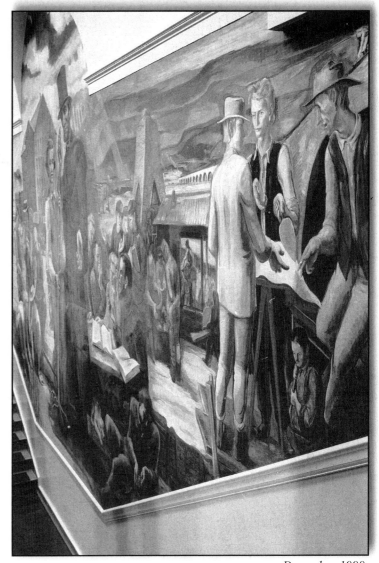

December 1998

Henry Varnum Poor at work on the main fresco

The Old Main Frescos are a major work of art by artist Henry Varnum Poor. He was helped by his daughter, Anne, who would apply the wet plaster in the morning before her father painted it. He painted it while it was still wet so that the paint and plaster would form a permanent bond. He began the actual painting in April of 1940 and finished the main work on June 18, 1940. In 1941 the senior, junior and sophomore classes voted to allot funds for more frescos in Old Main. The works were held up by World War II, and Poor began the second set of paintings in November 1948. He completed the work in June 1949. The entire work covers 1,300 square feet.

1929

The new President's Office, on the second floor of Old Main, soon after the construction of the present Old Main.

April 13, 1999

Today, the President's Office in Old Main is almost identical to the way it was, except for the furniture, the removal of the chandelier and the addition of the recessed lights in the ceiling.

circa 1931

Old Main foyer as it originally appeared before the small balcony was closed off and the fresco painting done.

December 1998

23

The coffee shop in the basement of Old Main around 1935.

The basement has been converted into a series of offices and cubicles.

circa 1915

Old Main, from the air, in this early photograph.

photo by John Elnitski Sr. circa 1990

1883

The view from the Old Main Bell Tower. Pugh Street is at left and Allen Street is at right, with College Avenue running across the middle of the photo.

April 14, 1999

Old Main today opens the Bell Tower a few times a year to the public.

The Nittany Lion

September 10, 1942

The finished Nittany Lion Statue with a broom and chips from its carving still at its base.

The term "Nittany Lion" is credited to Harrison D. "Joe" Mason, who lobbied for the use of the lion as the symbol of Penn State athletics. Mason was a member of the Penn State baseball team, visiting Princeton University in 1904. He was taunted with the symbol of Princeton--a Bengal Tiger. With his team having no symbol itself he made one up on the spot: the Nittany Mountain Lion. He assured his opponents that the Nittany Lions would overcome even the Tigers. They did. His idea to adopt the symbol for Penn State was an overwhelming success.

Easily the most photographed symbol of Penn State, the Nittany Lion still sits at its original site near Rec Hall. The idea of moving it has been discussed, but no decision has been made yet.

The class of 1940 voted to give its class gift ($5,430) to have a shrine constructed of the Nittany Lion. Sculptor Heinze Warneke carved the 13 tons of limestone in the summer of 1942 and it was ready for dedication during homecoming on October 24, 1942.

June 12, 1942

A 13-ton limestone block arrives at the site of the Nittany Lion.

July 21, 1942

Just a little more than a month after its delivery, the sculpture takes shape.

July 1942

The rough Nittany Lion emerges from the limestone. Warneke made a full-sized model of the sculpture, which is behind the original in this photo.

1942

Heinze Warneke soon after completing the Nittany Lion Sculpture.

Heinze Warneke returned to his sculpture, in November 1978, to repair an ear broken off by vandals. Warneke died in 1983.

May 1978

The most photographed symbol of Penn State, the Nittany Lion sculpture is always in demand on any graduation day.

October 1977

The Nittany Lion has had many types of visitors, including this baby lion.

The Obelisk

circa 1899

Built in 1896 by Michael Womer, a State College mason, the Polylith stands between Sackett and Willard buildings. However, it has also stood between the Armory and the Old Engineering Building. This display of Pennsylvania's building stones is the oldest monument on campus and has stood witness to all the changes the University has gone through. The Obelisk has never moved, no matter how many coeds passed by its delicate structure.

The 33-foot monument is made up of 281 stones gathered from 139 quarries, mostly in Pennsylvania. It is arranged geologically, so that the geologically older stones are at the bottom and the newer ones are at the top.

February 15, 1949

The Obelisk with the Electrical Engineering Building in the background.

December 12, 1998

Today the first building in the background is the Electrical Engineering Building East.

circa 1899

The Old Engineering Building, a large Romanesque-style building completed in the late 1880s. It was destroyed by fire in 1918.

1995

The Sackett Building behind the Obelisk.

1964

The Armory just before it was demolished in 1964.

circa 1904

January 1999

Willard Building is one of the main classroom buildings on campus.

The Cottages

circa 1889

The Commandant's house (later Pine Cottage). The children are, possibly, the children of Engineering Dean Robert Sackett, who lived in the house at the time.

In the University's early days, there were several cottages that were used primarily as residences for faculty. Later, in the 1920s through the 1940s, some were used for sororities and others were torn down. Today four cottages remain: three are located next to Ritenour Health Center: Birch, Spruce and Pine. The fourth, Ihlseng, is located next to Pattee Library. They are used for offices.

The original site of (left to right) Maple, Pine and Spruce Cottages is now Osmond Laboratory along Pollock Road. Pine and Spruce were moved. Maple was demolished in September 1955.

Osmond Laboratory.

1938

Pine Cottage, formerly the Commandant's house and later the home of Phi Mu Sorority is shown here passing Buckhout Laboratory on its way to its new home beside the Ritenour Health Center. The Cottage now houses the Artist Series Offices.

June 13, 1938

Spruce and Pine cottages sit at their new locations, beside Ritenour.

January 1999

Spruce and Pine cottages at their home for the last 61 years. Also, to the left of Spruce Cottage is Birch Cottage, hidden by the trees.

1965

January 1999

The last cottage to be removed was Oak Cottage in 1972. At the time it was the oldest building on campus, built for William G. Waring and his family in 1857. It was located beside Muller Laboratory behind Pond Laboratory. There was considerable protest over its demolition, but to no avail. The area is now a grass and sidewalk area that leads to Pattee Library.

Ihlseng Cottage, located next to Pattee Library, is named for its first occupant, Mining Dean Magnus Ihlseng. The residence was converted into an infirmary and opened for business in January 1915. In the first year it handled more than 11,000 patients.

1996

Today, Ihlseng Cottage houses the Institute for the Arts and Humanistic Studies.

The Armory

circa 1894

The Armory, built in 1892, housed social events, athletics and physical education classes. The building represented Penn State's commitment to military training required by the Land-Grant Act. This commitment was strongly based on the citizen soldier ideology. Before 1917, all male undergraduates were required to take Cadet Corps training.

January 1999

Today, Willard Building is one of the main classroom buildings for undergraduates.

circa 1941

The Obelisk and the Armory.

March 1999

The Obelisk and Willard Building.

circa 1958

The Armory and the Obelisk, before the demolition of the Armory in 1964.

September 1995

Willard Building and the Obelisk.

This formal dinner, in the Armory, celebrated the opening of the Main Engineering Building in 1893. Seated at the speaker's table, left center, is General James Beaver (chair pushed back). To Beaver's left is college President George Atherton, and seated to Beaver's right is Pennsylvania Gov. Robert Pattison.

1964

Despite considerable protest over the demolition, by faculty and students, the Armory was demolished in 1964 to make way for a new classroom building (Willard Building).

The Campus

1896

The Main Gate at College Avenue and Allen Street as it appeared in the late 1890s. Left is the old Engineering Building. The Armory and Obelisk are visible in the distance at center. The arc light, considered a great improvement at the time, hangs almost directly over the gate. In the foreground, at left, may be seen the iron loop which was part of the "trip gate" equipment. A buggy driver approaching the gate would steer the front wheel over the loop, thus opening the gate with a series of cables and weights. A similar loop was on the other side and the driver would again drive over it and close the gate. The old stiles and gateway were removed in 1897.

The Main Gate was closed to motor vehicles in 1924.

The Main Gate was a gift of the class of 1916.

December 1961

A low turnout during finals week at the Ice Skating Pavilion.

September 1995

The indoor track and field house at the Greenberg Sports Complex. This building was demolished in 1998.

circa 1930

Art class along Pollock Road facing Phi Gamma Delta fraternity.

April 1999

circa 1908

Dedicated on Feb. 22, 1893, the Main Engineering Building, across from the Corner Room, on the site of the present day Sackett Building, was considered one of the greatest achievements of the George Atherton era. The building marked a trend away from the purely agricultural school. The three-story, Romanesque-style building, designed by Fred L. Olds, with red brick and brownstone trim, was an impressive, state-of-the-art building. In 1893-94, 128 of the 181 undergrads were pursuing engineering degrees.

December 1998

Sackett Building now occupies the former site of the Main Engineering Building.

circa 1917

The Main Engineering Building and the adjacent Power Plant that generated steam and electricity for the campus.

December 1998

The Main Campus Gate, at College Avenue and Allen Street, with Hammond and Sackett buildings.

November 24, 1918

On the evening of Nov. 24, 1918, fire broke out at the rear of the Main Engineering building. The fire not only destroyed the building, but the Power Plant as well. Classes were canceled for several days until utilities could be restored.

1918

The loss was devastating to the University. It lost one of its most important structures and one of the most advanced engineering buildings in the country.

April 1961

Engineering Unit E behind Hammond Building.

September 1995

1960

The Penn State Creamery has always been a popular place.

March 1999

1903

Schwab Auditorium, built in the Beaux-Arts style of architecture, as seen from the second floor of the Botany Building. Schwab was the first building on campus built with money donated by Charles M. Schwab, president of Bethlehem Steel.

December 1998

Schwab Auditorium from the second floor of the Old Botany Building.

March 19, 1904

Students leaving Schwab Auditorium after Chapel. Schwab Auditorium was built because of the overcrowded conditions of the Old Main Chapel. The building was constructed for $150,000.

December 1998

Between classes near Schwab Auditorium.

1965

Schwab Auditorium steps on a sunny day.

September 1995

1952

Between classes along Pollock Road behind Schwab Auditorium.

February 1999

1971

The Museum of Art and the Visual Arts Building.

September 1995

Now, the Palmer Museum of Art after extensive renovation in 1993.

circa 1936

The Nittany Lion Inn under construction.

April 1999

Today the Nittany Lion Inn has 260 rooms for guests.

July 13, 1932

Built in 1930, the Mineral Industries Building replaced the old mining complex and represented a move away from a purely coal mining education to a more diversified mining education.

September 1995

The building was renamed for Edward Steidle, a key influence in changing Penn State into a state of the art facility in mining.

Year Unknown

R.O.T.C. drills across from Wagner Building.

April 14, 1999

Tennis courts across from Wagner Building.

January 11, 1952

The Art Gallery in the Mineral Industries Building.

February 1996

Steidle Art Gallery.

1954

In 1954 the Hetzel Union Building (H.U.B.) was a new addition to campus.

April 7, 1999

The new H.U.B., combined with the new Robeson Cultural Center, is scheduled to open in the fall of 2000.

1955

Even from the beginning, the H.U.B. fireplace room was a popular place to study, read the paper or catch a few winks between classes.

February 1996

1955

For decades the H.U.B. basement was filled with Ping-Pong tables and chess boards.

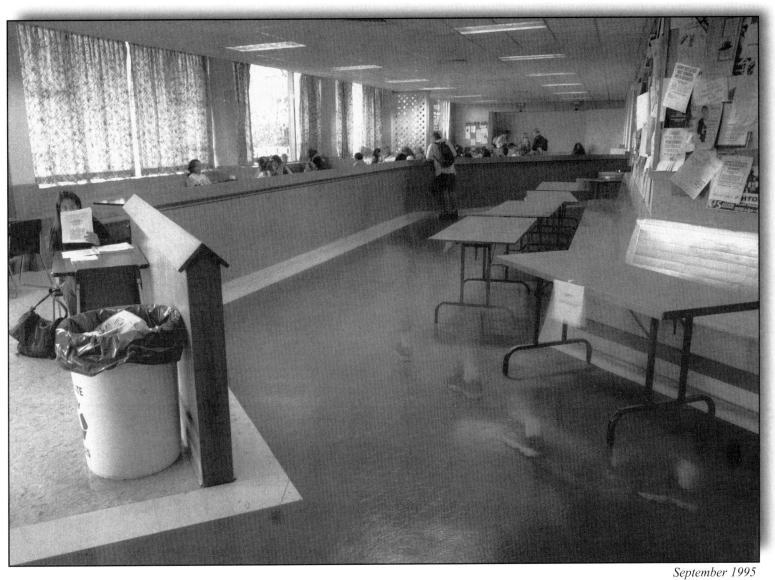

September 1995

The area was transformed into a space where student groups could display their ideas, on the tables to the right. The rest of the area contains tables and chairs for studying and eating. With the major renovation of 1999, this area no longer exists.

circa 1970

A popular place to eat and socialize in the H.U.B. was an extensive basement area, called "The Lion's Den." The juke box, at far left, was a constant source of music.

September 1995

The large open room was replaced with a variety of fast food areas and more seating. This area has since changed with the remodeling of the H.U.B.

1935

The main entrance to Borland Laboratory.

April 13, 1999

The Borland Laboratory entrance remains much as it was just after it was built.

A milk wagon waits at The Pennsylvania State College Creamery (Patterson Building) along what is now Curtin Road. Note the chickens running around in front of the building.

December 1998

1940

Electrical Engineering West Building Lobby and the Research Laboratory.

April 1999

Electrical Engineering West Building Lobby and the Electronic Materials and Processing Research Laboratory.

May 16, 1940

The President's House was the home to 11 Penn State presidents from 1864 to 1970. Eric Walker was the last to live there.

April 14, 1999

The oldest building on campus was to change again in 1999 as construction began for a new Alumni Center being added to the rear of the building.

1865

Built in 1864, the President's House was partially designed and financed by Penn State's first president, Evan Pugh.

April 1999

Today, the President's House houses the Alumni Association.

circa 1919

The Stock Judging Pavilion, built in 1915.

October 1995

Remodeled and renamed "The Pavilion Theatre," circa 1962.

Year Unknown

The Stock Judging Pavilion during an exhibition.

circa 1919

During World War I, the Stock Judging Pavilion was used as a training area for auto mechanics.

1927

In 1927, the Stock Judging Pavilion was host to the only Poultry Show in the world run by college students.

April, 13, 1999

Today, the Pavilion Theatre is host to plays and classes.

1952

Osmond Laboratory between classes.

December 1998

October 31, 1952

Whitmore Laboratory under construction.

February 1996

Armsby Building with a group of students on the steps.

circa 1938

Electrical Engineering Building under construction.

December 1998

Now known as Electrical Engineering West.

circa 1942

Pattee Library soon after its completion.

October 1995

1957

Pattee Library reading room for language and literature in Central Pattee.

December 1998

With construction in the main area of the Library, some of the computer and on-line services were temporarily moved into the study lounge. When renovated, this area will be the Diversity Reading Room.

1953

The second floor of Pattee Library was the main reference room.

December 1998

Today, it houses the maps collection. When current renovations are completed, this will be the Paterno Humanities Reading Room.

1951

The main entrance to Pattee Library.

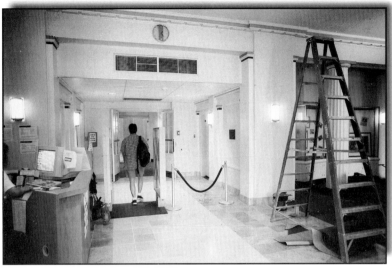

May 7, 1999

With the new marble floor in place, the new entry area takes shape during the library renovations.

circa 1975

The former east end of Pattee library.

May 7, 1999

With the major part of construction done, the Paterno Library is nearly complete on the east end of Pattee Library.

1928

Recreation Hall under construction. A tremendous amount of history has passed through the doors of this building.

February 1996

Rec Hall, as it is more commonly known, has been the site of numerous athletic events, graduations, concerts and other activities. Since the completion of the Bryce Jordan Center in 1996, Rec Hall has been less in demand. But it still hosts some athletic events and smaller concerts. In 1999, it hosted the Interfraternity Council Dance Marathon for the first time.

 *1935*

 *September 1995*

The main Rec Hall gymnasium before the suspended ceiling was added and the upper windows were closed off.

May 1930

Rec Hall interior soon after completion

September 1995

1961

Final examinations in Rec Hall

circa 1942

World War II drilling in Rec Hall.

Boxing filled Rec Hall at the height of the sport's popularity in the 1930s. Boxing remained a varsity sport until 1954.

1930

The graduating class of 1930 filled Rec Hall. Many thousands of students have graduated from here since then.

February 20, 1999

The first Interfraternity Council Dance Marathon to be held in Rec Hall since the marathon's inception. The Thon started in the H.U.B. Ballroom, moved to the White Building Gym and was held in Rec Hall in 1999. The Thon raised more than $2.5 million dollars for the Four Diamonds Fund, which benefits children with cancer. The Thon is the largest student-run philanthropy in the country.

circa 1890

The Agricultural Experiment Station soon after its construction in 1889.

April 13, 1999

Today, the Arts Cottage houses the Department of Visual Arts.

circa 1950

With a growing female population, Penn State constructed Frances Atherton Hall in 1938.

January 1999

121

June 5, 1950

Waring Hall under construction.

February 1999

1956

December 1998

Waring Hall entrance

circa 1953

February 1996

Waring Hall study lounge.

1955

The Waring snack bar was a popular meeting place.

December 1998

The area is still a popular place, though the computer lab doesn't serve malts or ice cream sundaes.

1948

The Colonial Georgian style residence halls, McElwain and Simmons, rise along Shortlidge Road. Each hall was designed to hold 1,000 female students.

February 1996

December 8, 1949

Thompson Hall in the West Halls complex under construction in 1949.

June 17, 1950

December 1998

September 20, 1965

The last of the dormitories of East Halls going up: left, Brumbaugh Hall; center, Pinchot Hall; and right, Tener Hall.

February 1999

December 8, 1949

McKee Hall under construction in 1949.

December 1998

circa 1960

Built in 1914, the Dairy Barn was destroyed by fire on Nov. 14, 1969. The Dairy Barn is also a literary landmark. Parts of John Barth's novel *Giles Goat-Boy* were inspired by the Dairy Barn.

January 1999

After demolition of the Dairy Barn, the Agricultural Administration Building was erected in 1971.

January 1, 1940

The first phase of Buckhout Laboratory, with the greenhouses under construction.

October 1995

May 10, 1930

Buckhout Laboratory, first floor General Laboratory.

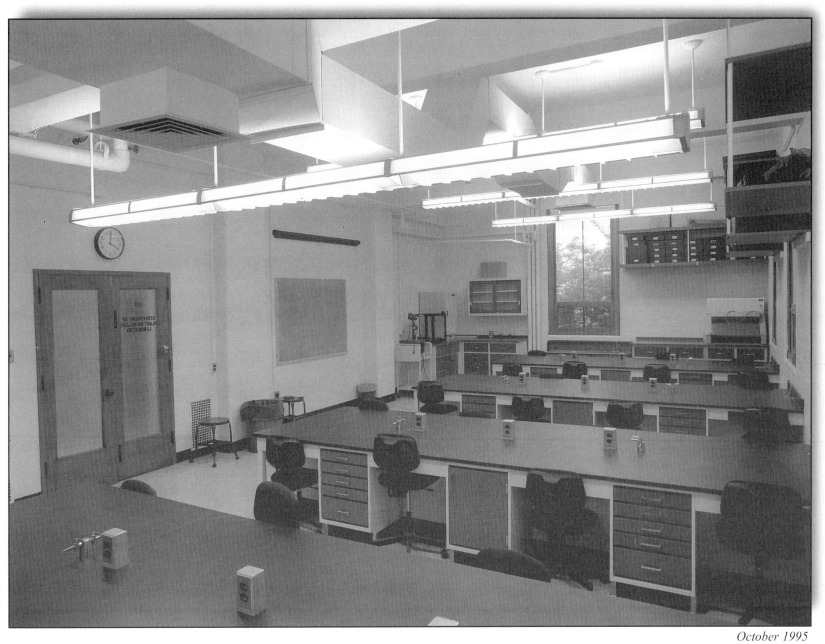

October 1995

Buckhout Laboratory room 103, Department of Plant Pathology Laboratory.

This photo, taken from a Chemistry & Physics Building window, was shot before the athletic field was named. Penn State's first football team (1887) played here. In 1893 the field was officially named Beaver Field and a 500-seat grandstand was erected, with a track and baseball diamond. The building on the left is the Agricultural Experiment Station. The small building, center, is the original Creamery, and the cluster of buildings on the right are the barns of Ag Hill.

April 1999

This photo was taken from Davey Laboratory. The Ag Experiment Station (Arts Cottage) is hidden left center behind the Frear Building.

A baseball game in progress at Old Beaver Field. The buildings are, from left to right, Maple Cottage, McAllister Building, the Chemistry & Physics Building (peeking out from behind is Old Main) and the Track House.

March 1999

Now most of the area is a parking lot. The buildings are, from left to right, Osmond Laboratory, Davey Laboratory, and Whitmore Laboratory. Future plans call for this area to become a courtyard.

1941

The grandstand at the new Beaver Field and the Water Tower, dedicated in 1909. The Nittany Lions beat Grove City 31-0 in the first game played there. After the 1959 season the Stadium was dismantled, moved to the present site, and reassembled with 16,000 additional seats.

November 1998

Now standing at the site is Nittany Parking Deck. The Water Tower was converted to become the Biomechanics Laboratory.

circa 1953

Beaver Field when it was near the center of campus along Park Avenue.

circa 1959

Beaver Stadium under construction in 1959. Dedicated Sept. 17, 1960, with a seating capacity of 46,284, Penn State beat Boston College 20-0.

Beaver Stadium with a record breaking crowd of 52,713. Penn State defeated West Virginia 20-0 on this day.

The first Big 10 football game at Beaver Stadium. Penn State defeated Minnesota 38-20 in front of 95,387 fans.

February 4, 1960

With the scoreboard in place, construction of the south end zone was complete.

November 1998

A 10,000-seat upper deck is planned for the south end zone, along with a three-level structure at the top of the east stands. The projects should be completed for the 2001 season opener. The seating capacity will be approximately 103,500.

April 14, 1960

The north end zone, from the scoreboard.

November 1998

The north end zone with the upper-deck stands that were built in 1991 to increase the stadium's capacity by more than 10,000 seats.

Downtown

circa 1896

Near the end of the last century, when this escaped pig roamed East College Avenue, little did anyone know that the pig would become the symbol for the Centennial Celebration held in 1996. A bronze pig and piglets now reside in the alleyway near the Tavern Restaurant to mark the celebration.

December 1998

East College Avenue. Below: the Centennial Sculpture by Eric Berg near the Tavern Restaurant.

The Pajama Parade aftermath: Back in the days when upperclassmen felt it their duty to harass the freshmen, the upperclassmen would choose a certain day, and then late at night ring the Old Main Bell to rouse the sleepy freshmen. The freshmen would be sent out to find all the buggies, barrels and any other kind of equipment that wasn't fastened down. It was all deposited at Co-op Corner (the corner of College and Allen). The following day, the owners would untangle their equipment and haul it home. This was the last Pajama Parade.

January 1999

May 1926

The "A" store at the corner of Allen Street and College Avenue.

March 1999

Today, Moyer Jewelers occupies the corner.

circa 1910

Looking down West College Avenue with the Corner Room on the left and the Engineering Building on the right.

March 1999

May 1926

The newly completed Cathaum Theatre on the 100 block of West College Avenue.

March 1999

The building was remodeled and the theatre was replaced by stores and offices.

1958

The Masonic Building, home of Kaye's Korner at the corner of Beaver Avenue and South Allen Street, has been a fixture in State College for decades.

October 1995

December 1998

1960

Construction of the University Drive overpass, in 1960, spanning East College Avenue.

March 29, 1999

1961

Paving of the eastbound lanes of the Benner Pike near the Duck Pond.

March 29, 1999

The State College Post Office at the corner of Beaver Avenue and South Allen Street. The Post Office moved to Fraser Street in 1965.

Schlow Memorial Library moved into the Old Post Office in 1967.

April 5, 1940

Near the intersection of Porter Road and Benner Pike, Centre Furnace played an extremely important role in the development of Penn State and State College. The iron furnace was built in 1790-91. It created growth and development for much of Central Pennsylvania. It was the offer by Centre Furnace owner James Irvin of 200 acres of land, and $10,000 donated by the citizens of Centre and Huntington counties, that ultimately brought Penn State to Central Pennsylvania.

November 1998

August 16, 1938

With the beginning of Atherton Hall, on the left, Shortlidge Road at College Avenue began to take shape. The old brick roadway that was College Avenue is clearly visible here.

February 1996

1978

The Wiener King at the corner of Calder Way and South Garner Street.

1999

Baby's Burgers and Shakes.

circa 1900

The 100 block of West College Avenue looking toward the main campus gate. Left to right are the Mechanic Arts Building, the Pump House, and the Gate House facing College Avenue.

March 1999

circa 1916

The Odd Fellows Building (I.O.O.F. 1032) on East College Avenue at the time of an Odd Fellows convention in 1916.

December 1998

The 100 block of South Allen Street.

circa 1925

The 100 block of West College Avenue from the Corner Room balcony. The Train Station is near the center, with the Engineering Units and the power plant to the right.

1960

Hammond Building stretches the length of the 100 block of West College Avenue.

April 14, 1999

The 100 block of South Allen Street, looking from Beaver Avenue to College Avenue. The horse and buggy are in front of the present day Omega Bank.

April 14, 1999

The 100 block of South Allen now hosts a variety of businesses and, possibly in the near future, a micro brewery.

With its red and white striped steeple, the Methodist Church was a State College landmark on the corner of what is now McAllister Street and East College Avenue. It was dedicated in 1888. The present stone church was erected on the same site in 1912.

circa 1951

St. Paul's United Methodist Church on the corner of
McAllister Street and East College Avenue.

February 1996

Gutted by fire on Nov. 13, 1987, St. Paul's United
Methodist Church was rebuilt. It opened again in 1990.

1934

Strubles Grocery from 1920-1958. From left to right: Robert Struble, Thelma Kline, George Kuhn, Ogle Kellerman, Charles Parsons, Don Cook and John Shank (driver).

October 1995

100 block of South Fraser Street.

circa 1900

Botany Professor William Buckhout's house at the corner of East Beaver Avenue and South Pugh Street. Buckhout was an avid photographer, and many of his early photographs are in this book.

March 1999

circa 1922

The State College Train Station, on campus, near the corner of Fraser Street and College Avenue. The station was removed in 1930.

January 1999

Possibly changing again, Hammond Building has been recommended for demolition in the next five years.

circa 1930

The Hotel State College at the corner of College Avenue and South Allen Street.

January 1999

The Hotel is still at the main crossroads of State College.

circa 1925

Passenger and freight trains arrived behind the present day Hammond Building and in front of the Engineering Units.

September 1995

Today that in-between area is used as a walkway and a delivery driveway. Rock climbers also use the vertical wall as a practice area.

State College Freight Station of the Bellefonte Central Railroad.

circa 1948

186

September 1995

Today, the building is the State College Bus Terminal.

May 1952

North Atherton Street construction at Woodland Drive. The work expanded the road from two lanes to four.

December 1998

Acknowledgements

A fee was paid to The Pennsylvania State University
Archives for publication rights to the archive photos.

Most of the information in this book came
directly from the photographs themselves.
However, I did reference and cross reference
the following sources. If you're interested in
Penn State History, I highly recommend them.

Penn State, an Illustrated History
by Michael Bezilla
Penn State Press 1985

The Nittany Lion
by Jackie Esposito & Steven Herb
Penn State Press 1997

History of St.Paul's Methodist Church
by Vivian Doty Hench 1952

Special Thanks

My biggest supporter. My right arm. My best friend. My wife:
Mindy Little

My inspiration. My center. My biggest hug. My daughter:
Natalie Little

My rock. My personality. My eyes. My teacher. My mom:
Audrey Little

My new family. My friends. My stepchildren:
Mandy, Jessica and Bobby Mitchell

A lot of effort was put into checking the accuracy of this
book. However, according to Murphy's Law, there are
bound to be mistakes. Please E-Mail me or write, so I can
correct the mistakes in future editions. Thank you.

How the book was done

Then and Now books have been around for a long time. It has always bothered me that the photos, in those books, always lacked the exactness I wanted to see. I thought that if you were going to compare two scenes across time, then those scenes should be compared precisely. That is why I came up with this system of seeing and shooting photos that are almost identical in perspective. I thought it would be of interest to you.

1. An extensive search through 100,000 Penn State Archive photos to find the original photos I wanted to use as my old photos.

2. Each original was carefully copied on T-Max 100 Black and White film.

3. The results, after film processing: an exact duplicate negative of the original.

4. These negatives were then cut and trimmed, so that the only piece remaining was the full frame part of the negative.

5. Negative and full-frame cut negative.

6. Now, I needed a camera with a removable prism. In this case a Nikon F5. I removed the prism.

7. I inserted the negative into the camera (backwards, and taped in) put the prism back on the camera. I used the same type of film I shot the copy negative with: T-Max 100 Black and White film.

8. Now, with the prism back on, the image rights itself and I can see this image through the lens. Then I locate the approximate angle the original was shot from.

9. When I look through the lens I can see both images and I move around until they line up as precisely as possible. This is harder than it seems. It takes a great deal of concentration and patience.

10. The results: a nearly identical set of negatives from many years apart. The images can then be printed. In this case the images were scanned into an Apple computer and then laid out on pages.

Order Form

All orders will be signed editions.

Quantity		Price	Amount
	Penn State Then and Now by Pat Little		
_____	**Hardcover Only**	$30 (each)	_____
	PA residents must add 6% sales tax ($1.80 per book)		_____
	Shipping and Handling......................... $4.95 (each)		_____
		TOTAL	_____

Photocopies or handwritten orders accepted.

Enclosed is my check or credit card information for the total amount shown.

Name _____

Address_____

City_____State____Zip_____

Phone (   )

Mastercard/Visa No._____

Exp. Date_____

Signature_____

<u>Mail to:</u>

Pat Little
P.O. Box 627
Lemont, PA
16851

Internet Orders:
www.patlittlephoto.com

Phone Orders:
814-235-8488